JOBS IN OUR COMMUNITY

LIBRARIANS
on the Job

By Mary Austen

KidHaven PUBLISHING

Published in 2017 by
KidHaven Publishing, an Imprint of Greenhaven Publishing, LLC
353 3rd Avenue
Suite 255
New York, NY 10010

Designer: Deanna Paternostro
Editor: Katie Kawa

Photo credits: Cover style-photographs/iStock/Thinkstock; pp. 5, 13, 23 wavebreakmedia/ Shutterstock.com; p. 7 andresrimaging/iStock/Thinkstock; p. 9 Wavebreakmedia/iStock/Thinkstock; p. 11 monkeybusinessimages/iStock/Thinkstock; p. 15 Purestock/Thinkstock; p. 17 Tyler Olson/ Shutterstock.com; p. 19 SW Productions/Getty Images; p. 21 Steve Debenport/iStock.com; p. 24 (library) Lester Balajadia/Shutterstock.com.

Cataloging-in-Publication Data

Names: Austen, Mary.
Title: Librarians on the job / Mary Austen.
Description: New York : KidHaven Publishing, 2017. | Series: Jobs in our community | Includes index.
Identifiers: ISBN 9781534521452 (pbk.) | ISBN 9781534521599 (library bound) | ISBN 9781534521575 (6 pack) | ISBN 9781534521582 (ebook)
Subjects: LCSH: Librarians–Juvenile literature. | Libraries–Juvenile literature.
Classification: LCC Z682.A97 2017 | DDC 020.92–dc23

Printed in the United States of America

CPSIA compliance information: Batch #CW17KL: For further information contact Greenhaven Publishing LLC, New York, New York at 1-844-317-7404.

CONTENTS

A library is a special place in a community. People go there to borrow books.

A person who works
at a library is called
a librarian.

A library has many books! Librarians help people find the books they want.

Libraries also have music and movies. Librarians help people find those things, too.

Librarians use computers. They show people how to use them.

Some librarians read stories to kids. Story time is fun!

A librarian lets people take books, music, and movies home.

18

You need a library card
to borrow things
from the library.

A librarian can help you get a library card.

Librarians are very helpful!